ALI'S STORY

A Real-Life Account of His Journey from Afghanistan

Editor: Michelle Hasselius
Production Specialist: Tori Abraham
The illustrations in this book were created digitally.

Picture Window Books are published by Capstone,
1710 Roe Crest Drive, North Mankato, Minnesota 56003
www.mycapstone.com

Library of Congress Cataloging-in-Publication Data
Library of Congress Cataloging-in-Publication data is
available on the Library of Congress website.
ISBN 978-1-5158-1412-2 (library binding)
ISBN 978-1-5158-1417-7 (eBook PDF)

Glossary

embarrassed (em-BARE-uhsst)—to
feel shame

frustrated (FRUHS-trey-tid)—to feel
hopeless or discouraged

helicopter (HEL-uh-kop-tur)—an aircraft
that can take off and land in a small space

mosque (MOSK)—a building used by
Muslims for worship

passport (PASS-port)—an official booklet
that allows a person to travel to
foreign countries

ALI'S STORY

A Real-Life Account of His Journey from Afghanistan

by Andy Glynne
and Salvador Maldonado

PICTURE WINDOW BOOKS
a capstone imprint

My name is Ali. This is the story of my
journey from Afghanistan.

My family and I lived in Afghanistan.
There were mountains and a lot of dust.
Most people weren't rich. They didn't have
houses. Instead, they lived in tents.

There was always fighting going on. The war started to get worse. There were a lot of helicopters in the sky. Tanks bombed our town and other cities.

Sometimes I
would look around and see
the fighting going on.
It made me very scared
but also really sad.

When we got to the airport, the officials let my grandma and me in. But they turned my mom and dad away.

The officials said that
my parents did not have
passports. They had to
go back home.

My grandma and I got on the plane. We thought my mom and dad were following behind us on another plane.

When we arrived in the new
country, we waited for the next plane.
My parents weren't on it.

My grandma and I were safe in this
strange new country. But we didn't know what
had happened to my mom and dad.
We felt alone and afraid.

Sometimes I'd dream that my mom would pick me up from school and walk me home.

Then I would wake up, and my grandma would be there instead. Then I'd realize it was all a dream.

It made me sad to think that my parents were back in Afghanistan with all the fighting and war.

I dreamed about them all the time.
I cried every night. It felt like the bones
in my body were broken.

Sometimes I felt angry. Most of the time, I felt really sad.

I learned a lot of new things at school. But it was really frustrating that I couldn't speak English. The only word I knew was ...

Sometimes I got
embarrassed when
I didn't know
the right word
for something.

In the beginning,
I sat in a corner of the
playground watching
all the other kids play.

Sometimes people would ask
me to play with them. Soon
I had a group of friends that I
played soccer with at school.

I really love drawing.
Everyone is amazed by my
pictures. Every day I draw
a special picture to show
people at school.

Sometimes it's a picture of
my whole family, just my mom
and dad, me, or a superhero.
(I really like superheroes!)

Four and a half years passed. Then one day we got a phone call.

My cousin said that he'd seen my dad praying in the mosque.

Then he handed the phone to my mom and dad. I talked to them for the first time in years.

It made me feel so happy.

My biggest wish is that my mom and dad will be able to come to this country.

It feels like it will happen
soon. I get upset when I
think about them. I wish
they could come right now.

I can't wait for that day.